PROPERTY INSURANCE EXPOSED

HOW TO NAVIGATE AND AVOID THE HIDDEN PITFALLS

JUSTIN CERNITZ AND
CANDISE SHANBRON

Property Insurance Exposed: How to Navigate and Avoid the Hidden Pitfalls

Published by Blue Ocean Publishing Group
Dunedin, FL

The information provided within this book is the author's personal thoughts and experience at the time of publishing. While we try to keep the information up to date and correct, there are no representations or warranties, express or implied, about the completeness, accuracy, reliability, suitability, or availability with respect to the information, products, services, or related graphics contained in this book for any purpose.

Contact: books@blueoceanpg.com

ISBN: 978-1-947436-06-0

Table of Contents

Introduction

When you have a property claim to a home or building, how do you know you are not being underpaid for your property damage or if a claim denial was justified? Is it possible that you are missing out on essential information that could help you receive the compensation you rightfully deserve?

When we sign up for insurance policies to protect our homes, buildings, and possessions, we trust that the insurance companies have us covered. We hope that if disaster strikes, we'll receive the compensation we deserve to rebuild and recover. But many people don't know that the insurance industry is not always as straightforward as it seems. Navigating the complex world of property insurance claims can be daunting, and policyholders are often left feeling overwhelmed and unsure of their rights.

Before I went to law school, my family faced an insurance claim for our Connecticut home. I remember being completely in the dark about the insurance claim process, and I had no idea my father might not receive the total compensation he was owed. We didn't know he had any recourse or options to fight back against the insurance company's decisions. Many years later, as an attorney specializing in insurance claims, I now understand the complexities of the industry and the importance of advocating for policyholder rights. I want to share my insights to help you avoid feeling lost and powerless, as my family once did.

In this revealing book, we aim to arm you with the information and insights that only a select few, such as lawyers and insurance professionals, typically possess. Our goal at Cernitz Law is to reveal the hidden secrets of the insurance industry that insurers would prefer you did not know. We will break down the details of property insurance claims so that you can make informed decisions and receive the compensation you rightfully deserve.

The insurance industry wishes to keep you in the dark about these essential insights, hoping that you will accept their decisions without questioning them and never challenge the decision or compensation they offer. However, you deserve to know the ins and outs of the process, successful strategies for navigating insurance claims, and how we fight back when you aren't being treated fairly.

A tell-all guide to the insurance industry, this book is custom crafted by lawyers who have dedicated their careers to helping policyholders navigate the complex world of property insurance claims. While there may be other resources available, we believe that this easy-to-understand guide stands out from the crowd and offers valuable insights and actionable advice.

We will explore the most common pitfalls and challenges that policyholders face when filing property insurance claims and discuss the importance of understanding your insurance policy and navigating the claims process. We will delve into specific issues like flood insurance, proof of loss requirements, and the unique challenges faced by policyholders, particularly in Florida.

Time is of the essence when it comes to understanding your rights and responsibilities as a policyholder. The sooner you learn about the intricacies of buying insurance, what is contained within your insurance policy, and the claims process, the better prepared you will be to face any challenges that may arise. With the knowledge and strategies shared in this book, you can avoid costly mistakes and ensure you receive the compensation you are entitled to when faced with a loss.

CERNITZ LAW

CernitzLaw.com

Chapter 1: Overview

Understanding How Insurance Works

A. You Need the Knowledge to Protect Yourself

Imagine standing on the edge of a cliff, gazing out at the vast expanse of life's uncertainties stretching out before you. It's a beautiful yet unsettling view. Your heart pounds, and you can feel the precarious nature of the ledge beneath your feet. This is where insurance steps in—providing a safety net to catch you if you fall.

But just like a safety net, insurance is only as strong and reliable as the knowledge you possess. You must understand the ropes, knots, and anchors holding the net together to ensure it will support you when it matters most. To protect yourself and your loved ones, you must arm yourself with knowledge of how insurance works and how to navigate the industry's complexities.

B. The Business Model of Insurance Companies

In the world of insurance, there's more than meets the eye. Beneath the surface lies a well-oiled machine designed to generate profits for insurance companies. This machine runs on two primary fuel sources: underwriting profit and investment income. Knowing how these sources work can empower you to make informed decisions and protect your interests while also understanding that insurance companies are in the business of making money.

First, let's discuss underwriting profit. Insurance companies assess risk and calculate premiums based on different factors depending on the type of insurance you intend to purchase. The goal is to gather enough premiums to cover the costs of claims and operational expenses. More importantly, to be able to invest in various investment vehicles.

Now, let's delve into investment income—the powerhouse behind the insurance industry. Insurance companies don't just sit on the premiums they collect; they invest them. By putting these funds to work in conservative assets like bonds, fixed-income securities, real estate, and stocks, they generate steady returns. This investment income is the lifeblood of the insurance business model and provides a stable, reliable source of profit.

While underwriting profit can ebb and flow, investment income remains a constant driving force. Insurance companies have built their business model around leveraging the wealth they accumulate from premiums to generate substantial returns through investments. This strategy highlights the fact that insurance companies exist primarily to make money.

As you navigate the world of insurance, remember that the majority of an insurer's profit comes from its investments, not just your premiums. Insurance companies are not non-profit organizations, and their primary goal is to maximize profitability.

C. Unmasking the Rigged Nature of the Insurance Industry

By now, we have established that insurance companies are profit-driven businesses, not benevolent non-profit organizations. Now, let's delve into how the insurance industry can be rigged against policyholders. Insurance companies cannot pay every claim in full, or they would face financial ruin. They meticulously manage their finances, employing actuaries and mathematicians to calculate reserves and strategically invest funds in real estate, stocks, bonds, and other companies. This investment-centric approach mirrors how banks operate, leveraging deposited funds to generate revenue.

Insurance policies, however, are often crafted using complex legal language, making them challenging to decipher for the average policyholder. Even attorneys with contract expertise may struggle to understand property insurance policies without specialized knowledge. Consequently, policyholders frequently need legal assistance to determine whether their insurer has treated them fairly, creating an inherent disadvantage.

Many policyholders wonder why their claims might be denied despite their timely and consistent premium payments. Remember, the insurance industry is not personal; its primary purpose is to accumulate and reinvest funds from policyholders. Insurance companies have a vested interest in minimizing payouts, which can result in denied or undervalued claims.

As you navigate the insurance landscape, keep this knowledge in mind and be prepared to seek professional help if needed. Armed with this information, you can better protect yourself and your loved ones in the face of life's uncertainties.

Chapter 2: Pitfall #1

Buying Insurance and Dealing with Insurance Agents

A. The Art of Selecting an Insurance Agent

The importance of choosing the right insurance agent and understanding the differences among agents cannot be overstated. Like any other professional or service provider, not all insurance agents are created equal, so properly vet your agent before purchasing insurance.

Licensing and Reputation

First, make sure your insurance agent is properly licensed and has no negative activity on their license, such as revocations or suspensions. Verify this information on your state's Department of Business and Professional Regulation website or other relevant licensing websites. Additionally, conduct a Google search on the agent and their agency to ensure there are no outstanding Better Business Bureau complaints or negative reviews.

Researching Insurance Agencies

An essential step, often overlooked by the general public but frequently employed by attorneys, is researching insurance agents and agencies through the Division of Corporations. This step can reveal important information and help uncover potential red flags associated with the principles of an insurance agency.

To conduct this research, visit sunbiz.org (if you are dealing with a Florida insurance agent) and enter the agency name to reveal the officers and directors. By searching for these officers and directors on the Division of Corporation website, you can uncover all corporations created by the principals of the insurance agency. If you discover a pattern of the same individuals opening and closing multiple insurance agencies under different names, it could signal suspicious activity.

In some cases, these individuals may set up shop next to, for example, a title agency or real estate agency, establishing a referral base to generate clients who need property insurance. Unscrupulous agents might pretend to procure insurance policies for these clients, even going as far as to create false declaration pages to give the appearance of legitimate coverage. In reality, they pocket the insurance premiums without providing actual policies.

Once they have collected enough premiums, they close the agency, move to a new location, and open a new agency under a different name.

This deceptive practice makes it challenging for consumers to seek recourse against the original agency, as most people lack the business savvy or knowledge to follow the trail or utilize available resources to uncover the truth. Therefore, it is crucial for individuals to thoroughly vet not only their insurance agent but also the insurance agency to avoid falling victim to such illegal schemes.

Shopping Around for the Best Coverage

After vetting the agent and the agency, it is important to remember that different insurance agents sell products from different insurance companies. Do not settle for the first option presented to you; always shop around with various insurance agencies to find the best coverage and pricing for your needs.

Some of the most important and common coverages you should have:

1. Windstorm, especially Hurricane, if you live in Florida.

2. Fire

3. Lightning

4. Vandalism

5. Plumbing losses (water damage)

6. Earthquake (if you live in geographic locations that have earthquakes)

There are many other coverages, depending on your geographic location and needs. The point is that whatever coverages are contained within your policy should be spelled out in writing by your insurance agent if you don't know how to read your policy. Likewise, you should put in writing to your agent the types of coverage you believe you need.

One of our clients encountered a highly questionable insurance agency that falsely informed her that no insurance company was willing to issue a policy for her home, except for one surplus lines insurance company. This deceptive tactic could be attributed to various incentive structures insurance companies offer, such as under-the-table deals or higher commissions to push specific products. While I won't delve into the specifics, it's essential to be aware of potential backdoor dealings and incentives that might be influencing an agent's recommendations.

Always seek a second opinion if you are not satisfied with the options presented or feel pressured toward a particular product or insurance company. Conducting due diligence will help ensure you receive the best coverage for your needs.

Captive And Non-Captive Agencies

There are two types of insurance agents: captive and non-captive. Captive agents exclusively sell insurance for a specific company, such as State Farm or Allstate. You can identify a captive agent by visiting their website or physical location, where you'll typically see only one insurance company's logo or branding.

In Florida, captive agents are typically construed to be agents of the insurance company they represent, acting on the company's behalf rather than the policyholders. Consequently, if a captive agent makes a mistake, their negligence may be attributed to the insurance company, and the policyholder can most likely seek recourse against the company. In contrast, non-captive agents, who sell products from multiple insurance companies, are likely to be construed as the policyholder's agents. If a non-captive agent errs, the policyholder most likely will not be able to seek recourse against the insurance company but may be able to pursue recourse against the agent.

In conclusion, properly vetting your insurance agent and agency is crucial to ensure you receive the best coverage and service. Research their licensing, agency history, and products they offer to make an informed decision. Finally, understand the differences between captive and non-captive agents to select the one that best suits your needs.

B. Mastering the Application Process and Steering Clear of Post-Loss Underwriting Pitfalls

Understanding the application process and avoiding post-loss underwriting practices is critical when dealing with insurance agents. This section will explore the importance of communicating with agents in writing and thoroughly reviewing the applications before signing them. Be aware that the defense of not understanding or not reviewing the application is not valid in Florida and perhaps true in most states.

Post-loss underwriting is a practice where insurance companies review your application after a claim has been filed, looking for any inaccuracies or misrepresentations. If they find any, they can deny coverage for your claim and potentially void your policy from its inception as if it never existed. Of course, they will have to refund your premium. To prevent this, you must ensure that you provide accurate information during the application process and work with a reputable insurance agent.

The Importance of Written Communication

Confirm every detail in writing, such as through e-mail, when buying insurance in person. Remember, if it doesn't exist in writing, it doesn't exist at all. When something goes wrong, you have better chances for legal recourse when you have a written record with your agent regarding the coverages you are seeking, as well as general information about yourself.

Reviewing the Application

A red flag should go up if the agent doesn't ask you any questions, instead presenting you with a pre-filled application and asking for your signature. But even if the agent does ask questions, you must remain vigilant. For example, the agent might inquire about your prior insurance claims. Suppose you have had two prior claims and disclose this information honestly. The agent may appear to note this down, but when the application is complete, they might not have recorded it accurately.

Why would an agent do this? Agents earn commissions by selling policies, and a candidate with multiple prior claims might not be an attractive risk for an insurance company. To secure their commission, an agent might falsify answers on the application to make a policyholder candidate appear more attractive. This is why you need to carefully review the questions and answers on the application before signing.

In states like Florida, you cannot claim ignorance or blame the agent for incorrect information on the application. Failing to review the application can lead to post-loss underwriting practices that not only void or deny coverage for your claim but also void your entire insurance policy, leaving you without any coverage.

A few examples below highlight the importance of not only providing truthful and accurate information but also carefully reviewing your insurance application to ensure that all information is accurate:

- A client purchased a house intending to rent it out and informed the insurance agent verbally about this plan. However, the agent failed to include this information on the application. The client did not review the application carefully and later faced a plumbing loss. The claim was denied, and the policy was canceled because the insurance company considered it a misrepresentation that the property was listed as the client's primary residence instead of a rental property.

- Another client truthfully informed their insurance agent about two previous insurance claims. The agent neglected to include these prior claims in the application. The client did not review the application before signing, and when they filed a claim later, it was denied, and the policy was canceled due to alleged misrepresentation.

- A client intentionally withheld information about their ongoing foreclosure proceedings and bankruptcy from the insurance agent. When they filed a claim, it was denied, and their policy was canceled for misrepresentation.

These examples emphasize the importance of carefully reviewing your insurance application before signing to ensure that all information is truthful and accurate. By doing so, you can avoid potential claim denials and policy cancellations due to misrepresentations.

Conclusion

Understanding the nuances of buying insurance and dealing with insurance agents is crucial to ensure you receive the best possible coverage for your needs. By carefully selecting a reputable insurance agent, thoroughly vetting the insurance agency, and mastering the application process, you can make informed decisions and safeguard your property and financial interests. Remember, knowledge is power, and conducting due diligence is essential to navigating the complex world of insurance.

At Cernitz Law, we understand how challenging this process can be and are here to help. If you need assistance navigating the various options available to you or require legal guidance related to insurance matters, don't hesitate to give us a call. Our experienced team is dedicated to protecting your interests and ensuring you have the coverage and support you deserve.

Chapter 3: Pitfall #2

Lender-Placed (Force-Placed) Insurance: A Costly Trap for Unwary Property Owners

Imagine receiving a letter from your mortgage company informing you that they have placed an insurance policy on your property because you failed to do so. You might breathe a sigh of relief, thinking that it is one less thing to worry about. But the reality is far from relieving. In fact, it could be a costly trap known as lender-placed (also referred to as force-placed) insurance. In this chapter, we will delve into the world of lender-placed insurance, the problems associated with it, and how to avoid falling into this trap.

A. The Hidden Dangers of Lender-Placed Insurance

Lender-placed insurance is a policy a mortgage company imposes on a property owner who has not maintained the required insurance on their financed property. While this may sound like a helpful service, it comes with several hidden dangers.

1. **Exorbitant Premiums:** Lender-placed insurance policies often carry much higher premiums than traditional insurance policies. This is because the lender chooses the policy, and the property owner bears the financial burden.

2. **Skimpy Coverage:** To make matters worse, these policies typically provide less coverage than a traditional insurance policy that the property owner could have chosen.

   Example: A client failed to pay for her insurance, so her mortgage company got a lender-placed policy to protect their interest in the home. However, the client did not realize that she was still responsible for paying for the lender-placed policy, and it had far less coverage than if she had purchased her own policy.

   Example: A client went into foreclosure, allowing his insurance to lapse. The mortgage company got a lender-placed policy to protect its interest. The client was still responsible for paying the high premium, and like in the first example, the policy had far less coverage, and he had little rights under the policy.

3. **Limited Rights for Property Owners:** With lender-placed insurance policies, property owners usually have little to no rights under the policy. In many cases, the property owner is not even considered an insured party and may have little to no recourse against the insurance company if the claim is either underpaid or wrongfully denied.

B. Lender-Placed Insurance: A Wolf in Sheep's Clothing

The process of lender-placing insurance often begins with an innocent-looking letter from the mortgage company. However, this letter rarely reveals the true nature of the lender-placed insurance policy, leaving property owners in the dark about the financial risks they face. Even when the proper and transparent information is reflected in the letter, these insurers are banking on a majority of folks to not fully review the contents of the letter or even understand the contents of the letter.

Unsuspecting property owners might assume that the mortgage company is looking out for their best interests. But, in reality, the mortgage company's primary concern is to protect its own financial interest in the property. Consequently, lender-placed insurance policies are designed to benefit the mortgage company, not the property owner.

C. In Conclusion: Do Not Fall Victim to Lender-Placed Insurance

Purchase and maintain your own insurance coverage: Property owners can avoid lender-placed insurance by maintaining their own insurance coverage. If a mortgage company sends a letter regarding lender-placed insurance, the property owner should immediately purchase their own policy to escape the pitfalls of lender-placed coverage.

Chapter 4: Pitfall #3

The Importance of Monitoring Insurance Policy Renewals

When it comes to insurance, many policyholders take a hands-off approach, believing that once they have a policy in place, they can sit back and relax. However, this mindset can lead to costly mistakes and leave you exposed to potential risks. One crucial aspect of managing your insurance policy is understanding the renewal process and its implications on your coverage. In this chapter, we will dive deep into the world of policy renewals, exploring the potential pitfalls and providing you with the knowledge you need to stay protected and proactive in managing your insurance.

Understanding the Insurance Renewal Process

Policyholders must understand the renewal process and the possible changes that may occur within their insurance policies. Many people take their insurance policy for granted, believing that if they have a policy in place, they are protected from all types of losses, and if they continue with the same policy, their coverage will remain the same. Unfortunately, this mindset can lead to unpleasant surprises.

Before getting into the renewal process, it is important first to make sure you understand what is covered and not covered under your policy.

When an insurance policy is renewed, policyholders often receive a renewal declaration page or policy documents, giving them peace of mind. However, this is where the potential for problems begins. Policyholders should make sure that the renewed policy contains the same terms and conditions as their previous one. Insurance companies may alter these terms and conditions upon renewal, often to the detriment of the policyholder.

A Cautionary Tale

In 2012, I encountered a case involving a client who had experienced a roof leak loss. The insurance company had exercised its alleged right to repair the property itself rather than pay money to the insured for their damages. The insurance company used a new endorsement, which I had never seen before in my years of practice, to limit the client's options for repair and potentially reduce the claim amount when the client had a policy that didn't allow the insurance company even to repair the damages. Upon further investigation, I discovered that this endorsement (which substantively changed the policy) was added to the policy midstream, which is not allowed under Florida law. My client never knew that the policy had changed or let alone that the insurance company had done so illegally.

My client only had $20,000 worth of damages at the most. However, because we discovered this illegality, the insurance company ended up paying a total settlement amount of $350,000.

The Notice of Change in Policy Terms Statute (for Florida residents)

Florida Statute 627.43141 requires insurance companies to provide clear notice of any changes to the policy terms upon renewal. However, this notice is often buried within the renewal package, making it difficult for policyholders to spot the changes.

Neither the regulatory bodies nor the courts have done anything to make the statute more stringent on the insurance companies to make things more obvious so that policyholders can more easily identify that changes are being made to their policy.

As a result, it is vital for policyholders to closely review their renewal documents, particularly the notice of change in policy terms. Failure to do so can lead to unexpected changes in coverage, possibly to the policyholder's detrimentt.

Even if you don't reside in Florida, there should be some type of regulation in the state you reside, requiring the insurance companies to provide proper notice of any changes made to insurance policies, especially if coverages are being reduced or taken away.

The Value of Legal Assistance

Many policyholders may not fully understand the changes to their insurance policy, even if they are aware of them. This is where law firms like ours come in. We assist policyholders in understanding the nuances of their policies, ensuring they know exactly what they are covered for and their rights.

Conclusion

Insurance policy renewals should not be taken lightly. Policyholders must be vigilant in reviewing their renewal documents to ensure that their coverage remains adequate to their needs and/or unchanged. By doing so, they can avoid potentially costly surprises in the event of a loss.

In summary, here are the key points to remember:

- Understand the insurance renewal process and its implications.
- Be aware of the potential for changes in policy terms and conditions.
- Seek assistance, if necessary, to fully understand your policy and your rights as a policyholder.

By keeping these points in mind and staying engaged in the renewal process, by monitoring any changes to your policy, you can help protect yourself from unexpected surprises should you have to make a claim.

CERNITZ LAW

CernitzLaw.com

Chapter 5: Pitfall #4

The Claims Process and How Insurance Companies Work

Imagine waking up to the sound of water gushing from a burst pipe or the crushing realization that your home has been destroyed by a hurricane. In these moments of chaos and devastation, you cling to the hope that your insurance policy will help you rebuild and restore your home. You have been paying your premiums, trusting that your insurance company will be there for you when the time comes should you have to make a claim. But as you embark on the claims process, you are suddenly met with roadblocks, delays, and confusing tactics that make it seem as if the insurance company is working against you rather than for you; however, by understanding how insurance companies work, you can successfully navigate these challenges.

In this chapter, we dive deep into the fourth pitfall of the insurance world: the claims process and how insurance companies operate. We'll uncover the tactics they employ to delay, minimize, and deny claims and provide valuable insight into how you can navigate this complex and often frustrating process.

The Ideal Claims Process

In a perfect world, the insurance claims process would be straightforward and hassle-free. You would report a loss to your insurance company, such as damage from a hurricane, a burst pipe, or a leaking dishwasher. An adjuster would promptly visit your property, assess the damage, and provide a fair estimate. The insurance company would then issue a payment within a reasonable period. Unfortunately, this ideal scenario is often far from the reality policyholders face when dealing with insurance claims.

The Crucial First Steps

When you experience a loss, act quickly to report the claim to your insurance company. Your policy may require you to report the loss as soon as possible. Failing to do so may give the insurance company grounds to deny your claim for late reporting of your claim.

In addition to reporting the claim, thoroughly document the damage to your property. Take photographs and videos of the affected areas to provide evidence for your claim and note any specific details related to the loss. This documentation will be invaluable when submitting your claim and during any subsequent negotiations or disputes. You need to have your own set of evidence because you cannot assume that your insurance company has accounted for all the damage.

Once you have reported the claim, the insurance company should assign a claim number and send an adjuster to assess the damages. The adjuster should schedule a visit at a convenient time for both parties and take photographs and measurements to estimate the damage. Ideally, the adjuster would also review your policy coverages with you and explain the process.

However, as we all know, the world is far from perfect, and the actual claims process can be fraught with delays, confusion, and frustration. In the following few pages, we will explore the realities of the claims process and how insurance companies operate, providing you with valuable insights to help you navigate this often-complex terrain.

The Reality: Delays and Challenges

Unfortunately, the claims process is rarely as smooth as we would like. Adjusters may not communicate effectively with homeowners, and insurance companies often employ delay tactics to avoid paying out claims. These tactics can include:

1. **Switching desk adjusters:** A desk adjuster/examiner is your main point of contact at the insurance company for your claim. If the insurance company switches desk adjusters several times, this practice leads to confusion and delays, making it difficult for policyholders to keep track of who is handling their claims.

2. **Making it difficult to communicate with the insurance company:** There are instances where the insurance company makes it difficult to communicate in a transparent manner. For example, the insurance company may refuse to provide any e-mail addresses, forcing the insured's only option for communication via telephone, which makes it impossible for any record-keeping to prove that a communication occurred or what the communication entailed, leaving you with no proof. Other insurance companies may request you to communicate through an online portal via their website, which also makes it challenging for you to have the necessary proof that something was provided to them or that a communication occurred.

3. **Requesting irrelevant documents:** Insurance companies may ask for documents, information, or records that have no bearing on the current claim, further delaying the process.

4. **Conducting examinations under oath:** This tactic can be used to intimidate or harass policy-holders, forcing them to spend hours recounting details of the incident and their property. It may be used when insurance companies suspect fraud or believe a policy-holder has not disclosed essential information.

5. **Denying claims based on inaccurate information:** Insurance companies may deny claims even when evidence is presented that supports the policyholder's case. For example, a claim may be denied based on a weather report stating that there was no hailstorm, even when the policy-holder was smart enough to have video evidence of the storm.

6. **Underpaying claims:** Insurance companies often issue lowball payments in the hope that policyholders will accept the amount and not pursue further action. This tactic saves the insurance company money in the short term but

can leave policyholders without the necessary funds to repair their property.

Understanding the Insurance Company's Perspective

It's essential to remember that insurance companies are businesses, and their primary objective is to protect their bottom line. While it may feel personal when a claim is denied or delayed, policyholders must understand that they are just one of many customers dealing with similar issues. Insurance companies are not targeting specific individuals; they are trying to maximize profits.

This profit-seeking behavior is driven by the need to satisfy shareholders, maintain financial stability, and invest in future growth. The insurance companies work to minimize claim payouts and maximize profits. This strategy ensures that the insurance company remains profitable and able to continue providing coverage to its policyholders.

By understanding the insurance company's perspective and motivations, policyholders can better anticipate potential challenges and develop strategies to navigate the claims process effectively.

Navigating the Claims Process Successfully

To successfully navigate the claims process and ensure you receive the compensation you deserve, consider the following steps:

1. **Stay organized:** Keep detailed records of all correspondence with the insurance company, including phone calls, e-mails, and letters. Maintain a file with all relevant documents, such as policy information, damage reports, photographs, and receipts. It's best to communicate with the insurance company in writing.

2. **Remain proactive:** Follow up with the insurance company regularly – in writing, to check on the status of your claim. Keep track of deadlines and make sure you submit any requested information and documentation promptly.

3. **Seek professional help:** If you are struggling to navigate the claims process or believe your claim is being handled improperly or unfairly, consider consulting with an attorney who specializes in insurance claims. These professionals can provide valuable guidance and support throughout the process.

While the insurance claims process can be challenging and frustrating, understanding how insurance companies operate and taking a proactive approach can help you navigate the process more effectively. By staying organized, seeking professional help when needed, and knowing your rights, you can increase your chances of receiving the compensation you deserve for your property damage.

Also, with the information in this booklet, you will hopefully learn to manage your expectations. Even if you think you have done everything right, your claim may still be denied or underpaid. Don't take it personally. This is the business of insurance, after all.

Chapter 6: Pitfall #5

Policy Requirements and Conditions Precedent

Imagine discovering extensive water damage in your office building, only to realize that your insurance claim might be denied because you were unaware of the damage for months or even longer. This is just one of the challenges policyholders may face when dealing with policy requirements and conditions precedent.

Conditions precedent are specific requirements or actions that must be fulfilled or completed before an insurance company is obligated to provide coverage or pay out a claim. Post-loss conditions are the obligations and duties of the policyholder after experiencing a loss and submitting a claim.

In this chapter, we will explore the critical post-loss conditions, common pitfalls, and strategies for successfully navigating these requirements to ensure you receive the coverage you deserve.

Understanding Post-Loss Conditions

Insurance policies typically include provisions outlining the policyholder's responsibilities after experiencing a loss and submitting a claim. Some common post-loss conditions include:

- Providing timely notice of a loss.
- Allowing the insurance company to inspect damage.
- Granting access to books and records.
- Complying with requests for recorded statements or examinations under oath.
- Submitting a proof of loss.

It's essential to thoroughly review your policy to ensure you understand your obligations. Each insurance company may have specific requirements and conditions that you need to follow.

Throughout our work as property claims lawyers, we have taken over cases from prior lawyers who did not know what they were doing and filed a lawsuit without having the client first comply with different policy conditions under the insurance policy. In those cases, the client had an uphill battle or lost the case because of a failure to comply with policy conditions, like a failure to submit a proof of loss, the failure to submit to an Examination Under Oath, and instances where a client repaired damages or replaced the roof before the insurance company could inspect the damages. In the latter case, the client lost because the insurance company was prejudiced by not having an opportunity to inspect the damages. These examples underscore the importance of understanding and adhering to policy requirements and conditions precedent to successfully navigate the claims process.

Timely Notice

A policyholder is responsible for providing timely notice of a loss. Failing to do so could result in the insurance company using a late notice defense to deny coverage.

Challenges with Late Notice

Imagine Hurricane Ian struck on September 28, 2022, and another hurricane hit on January 4, 2023. If you report damages from Hurricane Ian in February 2023, the insurance company might argue prejudice, claiming they cannot verify the damages' origin. This is especially problematic if you have a new insurer by January 2023, as your old insurer would be responsible for the damages from Hurricane Ian.

Another example is when a policyholder reports damages a year or two after the event, it becomes challenging to prove that the damages are attributable to that specific loss.

Examinations Under Oath and Recorded Statements

If the insurance company requests an examination under oath or a recorded statement, you should understand the difference between these two processes. An examination under oath is a formal process involving a court reporter and, often, a lawyer. A recorded statement is an informal, recorded conversation with an insurance adjuster. If an examination under oath is requested, it's wise to seek legal counsel to ensure you are properly represented and not taken advantage of.

Be aware that insurance companies can sometimes use the formal nature of an examination under oath to intimidate policyholders. While there may be legitimate reasons for requesting an examination under oath, there are instances where it is used as a scare tactic rather than for genuine purposes. In such situations, consulting with a lawyer can help determine whether the examination under oath request is warranted or is being used to intimidate the policyholder. Being mindful of this possibility can empower policyholders to make informed decisions and seek legal advice when necessary.

Policyholders should prepare for these procedures by gathering relevant documents, creating a timeline of events, and being honest and forthcoming with the information provided.

The Importance of Proof of Loss

A proof of loss is a document in which the policyholder attests to the amount of their claimed damages. This document is usually required to be notarized and is used to inform the insurance company of the amount of the loss being claimed. Failing to submit a proof of loss when requested can result in a denial of coverage.

Flood Insurance and the National Flood Insurance Program (NFIP)

This key section on policy requirements and conditions precedent highlights the importance of understanding proof of loss requirements, particularly in relation to flood insurance carriers.

Most insurance policies require policyholders to submit a proof of loss only if the insurance company requests it.

However, there are exceptions that can catch policyholders off guard. These exceptions are especially important to consider when dealing with flood insurance.

Flood insurance is typically underwritten by the National Flood Insurance Program (NFIP), and because of this, flood policies almost always have an automatic proof of loss provision. In flood claims, policyholders must submit a proof of loss even if the insurance company doesn't request it. This can be problematic, as many people are unfamiliar with their insurance policy's content and how to read it.

Numerous lawsuits involving legitimate flood claims have been dismissed due to the failure of the insured to submit a proof of loss. So, policyholders dealing with flood claims must be aware of this requirement.

Navigating Policy Requirements and Conditions Precedent

Successfully navigating policy requirements and conditions precedent is crucial to ensure you receive the coverage and compensation you deserve after experiencing a loss. By understanding your responsibilities, communicating with your insurance company, and seeking legal counsel, when necessary, you can avoid potential pitfalls and challenges in the claims process.

The key points to consider when navigating policy requirements and conditions precedent include:

- Familiarize yourself with your insurance policy and its conditions precedent.
- Provide timely notice of a loss and establish clear communication with your insurance company.
- Be prepared to submit a proof of loss.
- Seek legal counsel if facing an examination under oath or when encountering challenges in meeting policy requirements.
- Stay organized and keep detailed records of all damages, expenses, and correspondence related to your claim.

By keeping these strategies in mind, you can navigate policy requirements and conditions precedent effectively and ensure that you receive the insurance coverage and compensation you are entitled.

There may be other requirements in your insurance policy that you may need to comply with, so all policyholders should familiarize themselves with the policy conditions provision of their policy. In the event of a loss and filing a claim with your insurance company, knowing your duties and responsibilities is essential.

Consider reviewing your policy with a trusted attorney who can help you understand the complexities of your policy and any specific requirements.

Chapter 7: Seeking Legal Help

The Key to Leveling the Playing Field

When faced with insurance claims, you may need a strong legal ally by your side. In this chapter, we'll explore the importance of seeking legal help and how partnering with a specialized property claims attorney can level the playing field, ensuring you have the best chance of receiving the compensation you deserve.

Going Solo is Not Always the Best Option

Imagine trying to solve a complex puzzle or navigate a challenging maze without any guidance or assistance. The countless twists, turns, and dead ends can leave you feeling frustrated and defeated. This is the reality of dealing with insurance companies on your own.

Insurance companies have vast resources, industry expertise, and legal teams at their disposal. As a policy-holder, it's easy to feel outmatched and overwhelmed. But fear not, for there is a way to level the playing field: seeking legal help. Enlisting the aid of an experienced property insurance attorney can provide you with the guidance, support, and firepower you need to stand your ground and advocate for your rights.

The Importance of Specialized Legal Expertise

Navigating the world of insurance claims requires more than just a passing familiarity with the law. Just as you wouldn't consult a dermatologist for a heart condition, you need a lawyer who specializes in property claims when facing insurance disputes.

Property claims law is a unique and intricate field, teaming with specific knowledge, facts, and strategies that general legal practitioners may not possess.

By partnering with a law firm like Cernitz Law that specializes in property claims, you ensure that your case is in the hands of professionals with a deep understanding and experience. This expertise is invaluable in helping you build a strong claim and successfully counter the tactics employed by insurance companies, ultimately saving you time, and minimizing stress.

The Risk-Free Advantage of Working with Cernitz Law

At Cernitz Law, we understand the challenges policyholders face when dealing with insurance companies, especially since we used to represent the insurance companies and know their games. We are dedicated to providing specialized legal support tailored to your needs.

We do not charge our clients an hourly fee for property damage claims. We offer a contingency-based approach, meaning you won't pay out of pocket for our services. Instead, our fees come from a percentage of the settlement we secure from the insurance company on your behalf.

This risk-free arrangement ensures that our interests are aligned with yours. We are motivated to fight for the best possible outcome, as our success is directly tied to yours. By working with Cernitz Law, you can rest assured that you have a formidable ally in your corner, committed to helping you navigate the insurance wilderness and secure the compensation you deserve.

Addressing Concerns and Misconceptions

Some policyholders may feel apprehensive about seeking legal help, believing they can handle the claim process on their own or worrying about the costs involved. Others might be concerned that involving a lawyer could slow down the claims process or create a more adversarial relationship with the insurance company. However, it's important to recognize that the expertise and support offered by a specialized attorney can prevent costly mistakes, streamline the process, and significantly improve your chances of a successful outcome.

The Power of Real-Life Examples

Real-life examples emphasize the importance of seeking legal help. In numerous cases, we have successfully overturned denied claims and obtained additional monies where a claim was underpaid. For example, one client was initially paid $82K by their insurance company for hurricane damages. We pursued legal action and ultimately secured an additional $750K for them.

In another case, the client's real estate broker and insurance agent assisted her in purchasing an insurance policy for a house she was closing on. Unbeknownst to her, the policy contained a wind exclusion. Under normal circumstances, there would have been no way to help her, and most attorneys would have quickly and automatically turned the case down. However, something didn't seem right, so we continued probing her with questions and requested more documentation, as our instincts told us something was amiss.

By taking the time to ask questions and review extensive documentation that most lawyers would have overlooked, we were able to uncover a major conspiracy. As a result, our client received $50K in compensation that she would never have received if she hadn't come to Cernitz Law.

Cernitz Law recently settled a condominium association's hurricane claim for $5,000,000 when a prior lawyer for the condominium association was unable to obtain coverage or a single dollar because the condominium association reported the claim more than two years after the hurricane damaged the entire property. But through the expertise of the lawyers at Cernitz Law, a very successful $5,000,000 outcome was achieved.

By partnering with a specialized property claims law firm like Cernitz Law, you gain access to invaluable expertise, a risk-free contingency-based approach to representation, and the assurance that you are not facing the insurance giants alone. With the right legal team by your side, you can level the playing field and confidently pursue the justice and compensation you deserve.

CERNITZ LAW

CernitzLaw.com

Conclusion

Empowering Yourself to Face the Insurance Giants

As we reach the end of our journey through the intricate world of insurance, it's essential to reflect on the insights we have gained and the empowerment that comes with knowledge. With a newfound understanding of the insurance landscape, we can now face the challenges ahead with confidence, determination, and unshakable resolve to protect our interests and those of our loved ones.

Throughout this book, we have unraveled some of the complexities of the insurance industry, delving deep into its profit-driven business model, the often-unfair nature of the system, the possibilities of dealing with bad actors in the industry, having to comply with certain requirements under the insurance policy, and the importance of seeking specialized legal help. We have learned that insurance companies are not benevolent entities; they exist to make money and protect their interests, sometimes at the expense of policyholders.

But there is hope. Armed with the knowledge we have gained, we can better advocate for ourselves, make informed decisions, and seek out the right legal help to level the playing field. By understanding the insurance landscape, we can navigate its challenges with confidence and determination.

In the face of life's uncertainties, we are now better equipped to protect ourselves and our loved ones from the pitfalls and perils that lurk beneath the surface. This book has provided you with some tools and the ability to stand up to the insurance giants and ensure you have the best chance of receiving the fair and just compensation you deserve.

As you venture forth into the world of insurance, remember the lessons you have learned here. Be vigilant, be informed, and be unafraid to seek help when needed. Put the knowledge you have gained into practice and know that our team at Cernitz Law is just a call away, ready to provide guidance and support. Together, we can conquer a myriad of challenges faced when dealing with the insurance companies and/or other issues in the insurance industry.

About Cernitz Law

Cernitz Law, a well-known and respected boutique law firm with over six decades of combined legal experience serving Florida, prides itself on delivering the highest caliber of legal representation to clients from all walks of life. The firm's attorneys have won thousands of legal victories for homeowners, commercial property owners, condominium owners, individuals who have suffered injuries, and people and businesses navigating a range of commercial/business disputes. The team at Cernitz Law brings extensive knowledge, experience, gumption, and passion to every challenge, ensuring every client receives the best possible representation.

What truly sets Cernitz Law apart is its unique process. The firm believes in being not just aggressive advocates for their clients but also problem solvers. This approach is akin to a doctor treating the underlying cause of an illness rather than merely addressing the symptoms. Cernitz Law operates on a collaborative model, where all attorneys are involved in each case as a team. They regularly engage in roundtable discussions, which helps in developing the best strategies to achieve optimal outcomes for their clients.

At Cernitz Law, the team believes that "the devil is in the details," and they leave no stone unturned when evaluating and prosecuting their cases. This meticulous approach, combined with their personal investment in every case, is why they treat each client's case as if it were their family's or their own. It's this dedication and commitment to their clients that sets Cernitz Law apart, ensuring that every client receives the representation they deserve.

"They're Going to Fight for Your Rights"

Kevin Harrington – the original "Shark"
from the hit show Shark Tank

"If you're looking for a trustworthy and professional legal team to guide you through a difficult time, dealing with a hurricane, a storm, or any type of loss that causes damage to your property, you need to check out Cernitz Law.

With years of experience, their team is dedicated to helping clients get the compensation they deserve for property damage. They know the ins and outs of property damage law, and they're going to fight for your rights.

They used to represent the insurance companies, so they know the games that they play, and they have a unique vantage point. They work tirelessly to make sure that their clients get the best possible outcome for their case."

"Our Lives Have Become Much Happier"

Rodolpho Solares Jr.

"The mold inside the walls was so extensive that we had to shut down the bathroom for about two years. This situation forced everyone to use the same bathroom, which significantly impacted our lives.

Once the Cernitz Law Firm got involved, they rectified everything that was wrong with the bathroom.

A couple of years later, Hurricane Irma hit Miami, causing damage to my house. Remembering their previous helpfulness, I thought about reengaging with the Cernitz Law Firm.

I'm glad I made that decision because it enabled me to get the necessary repairs done to my home. Since working with the Cernitz Law Firm, our lives have become much happier."

"We Were Able to Successfully Restore the Property"

Rosa Ramos

"I inherited a home from my parents, a place that had been rented to a family. One day, we received a call informing us that the house was on fire and burning down.

All I could think about was how this house was one my mother had taken care of so lovingly. Arriving on the scene and witnessing its condition was truly heart-breaking.

However, once I contacted Cernitz Law, a great load was lifted from me. We were able to successfully restore the property, and now, it looks beautiful, honestly."

"Extremely Supportive and Provided Guidance"
Roberta Marcus

"I manage the Marcus Center in Miami, Florida, which comprises 52 offices and accommodates 52 tenants. Our building was affected by a lightning strike and fire, disruptions which significantly impacted our day-to-day operations and our ability to manage the property.

In order to restore the building and ensure our tenants' welfare, we had to pay out of pocket. We filed a claim and believed we had provided all necessary documentation for its approval. However, we received a letter informing us that our claim wouldn't be covered.

Throughout this process, Justin from Cernitz Law was extremely supportive and provided guidance. We were able to reach a settlement with which I was comfortable.

When choosing legal representation, it's important to find someone who will do the best job not only for you personally, but also professionally. With Cernitz Law, we found exactly that."

"They Managed to Win My Case"

Salvadore Blanco

"We experienced a hurricane accompanied by ten intense days of rain. The result was a destroyed kitchen. That's when the battle began. The insurance company informed me they wouldn't cover the damage.

That was until Cernitz Law became involved. They managed to win my case."

Made in the USA
Monee, IL
04 November 2026

67380151R00039